Spiritual Insights of T. W. Willingham

Book 7

Crumbs That Challenge the Saints

Part 2

Crumbs That Challenge the Saints

Part 2

Beacon Hill Press of Kansas City
Kansas City, Missouri

ISBN: 083-411-1675

Printed in the
United States of America

Cover design: Crandall Vail

10 9 8 7 6 5 4 3 2 1

Contents

Foreword

Dr. T. W. Willingham is almost a legend in the Church of the Nazarene. He has served as pastor, district superintendent, college president, and executive at the world headquarters of the church.

Somewhat like Bernard Baruch he has been a close advisor to general superintendents and fledgling executive directors over the years. His business acumen and practical judgment have been sought after by all of us.

His greatest impact, however, has been in the spiritual realm. I and literally thousands have been stimulated by his insight into the Scriptures. Take these "crumbs," which I consider the most prophetic (prophetlike) pieces that have ever come from our presses, and revel in them.

—M. A. (BUD) LUNN

A Note of Thanks

First, I desire to thank my God for giving me time, strength, and guidance during the past 40 years as I have worked on the 16 books that I have had published.

In 1970, the Lord gave me a five-page directive concerning my writings in which He said, "I have given you two helpers . . . and it is My desire that they help you, and if they abide near Me they will feel the same way."

These two God-given workers—Clara Rogers and Kathy Butts—have been dependable and efficient and, more important, have felt that in so laboring they have been serving the Master and His kingdom.

Clara has corrected nearly all my handwritten articles, as well as typing many. Kathy has typed much, organized material, and by research and study, has made many valuable contributions. I thank God for both of them; without such help my work could not have been done.

If these messages prove to be of spiritual help to you, just give all the praise to our Heavenly Father.

—T. W. WILLINGHAM

Holiness Does Not Establish One

Volumes have been written on holiness and what it will do for the one obtaining it; so a few lines on what it will *not* do may be in order.

Holiness does not establish one. This truth should be pointed out, for often have I heard it preached that it would do so. It has often been called the "establishing grace," but that is not true; the Bible does not teach it, and life does not sustain it. Much harm has been done by overstating, or incorrectly stating, what any work of divine grace will do.

If it still be insisted that holiness establishes one, we can answer that holiness is necessary that we may become established; but by the same token, it can be said that regeneration, or conversion, is necessary for one's establishment. Certainly no sinner can be established in grace, nor can an unholy person become established. In that sense both regeneration and sanctification are needed as a basis for establishment, but neither establishes one.

The record is, "After that ye have suffered a while, [He will] make you perfect, stablish, strengthen, settle you" (1 Pet. 5:10). Suffering a while, and receiving the sanctifying power of God in a moment of time, are two separate things and are accomplished by different time schedules. Time is necessary for suffering, and suffering must precede establishing.

The same truth is taught in Hebrews where the writer is contrasting the "babe" in Christ with those "of full age." One can only become of full age by having his "senses exercised to discern both good and evil" (5:13-14), and it takes time to exercise one's senses.

The time element necessary for perfection is seen in the life of Christ. It was necessary "to make the captain of their salvation perfect through sufferings" (Heb. 2:10). Then there came a time (after His sufferings) that it could be said of Him, "And being made perfect, he became the author of eternal salvation" (5:9).

Much harm has been done by claiming for some work of divine grace more than God teaches, and this teaching that holiness establishes is such a false doctrine. It contradicts the Word.

Many young Christians, having been thus taught, and finding themselves unsettled after sanctification, begin to doubt their experience, become discouraged, and give up the race. It takes a lot of suffering to bring the newborn Christian to strength and stability of Christian character.

It should also be noted that God has promised to establish one. One need not fear and despair at this point. It is just that we need to know the method by which this is to be done and not be misled and become disillusioned, when we are, in fact, in the process of becoming established.

The laws of grace are in many ways like the laws of nature. Why not? God established both. First, we have the seed, then the sprout, the stalk, the ear, and then the ripened grain. We have the helpless babe, the growing child, the maturing youth, then the full grown.

In all of God's natural workings, time is required; so in grace. We need not be discouraged if although saved and sanctified, we find ourselves not established. We are on our way, but times of suffering are needed. That was true of the Christ who "learned . . . obedience by the things which he suffered" (Heb. 5:8), so we can learn in no other way.

While holiness does not establish one, it is a necessary

prerequisite; so is conversion; so is conviction. Each of these have its place, but all of them together cannot establish one. Time and suffering are required.

Such facts do not in any way minimize the value and the necessity of being holy, for "without [holiness] . . . no man shall see the Lord" (Heb. 12:14). It merely puts it in its proper place.

To claim more for anything than is true is to do damage to truth and to the things for which the untrue claim is made.

If it is our sincere desire to become grown-up and established, we should not turn to the altar for a crisis experience to accomplish this, but rather rejoice when the means of establishing are being encountered. Perhaps it was this point Peter was making when he wrote, "Think it not strange concerning the fiery trial . . . but rejoice" (1 Pet. 4:12-13).

James was saying the same thing: "Count it all joy when ye fall into divers temptations . . . the trying of your faith worketh patience" (1:2-3).

Trials and tests are more easily borne when one realizes that they are the inevitable and necessary stepping-stones to stability, and not proofs that he has fallen from grace or that he has never had the "blessing."

If one can but see that life's tests are gateways to perfection, he can begin to understand why Peter could say, "But rejoice," and James enjoin, "Count it all joy." One may learn to be happy in the process, for the process procures peace.

To understand here is to give zest to the Christian way and find the bow of promise draping life's darkest clouds. There is no place for somber sadness in the Christian life, for there is this assurance that "our light affliction, which is but for a moment, worketh for us a far more exceeding and eternal weight of glory" (2 Cor. 4:17).

Let us then become followers of Christ, enter into the way of holiness, and faithfully suffer with Him to gain the stability and strength of the "full grown."

Jesus Knowing . . . He Was Come from God . . . Took a Towel

(John 13:3-4)

The story of Jesus washing the feet of the disciples, when the disciples felt it below their dignity to do so, has often been told and bears many repeatings, but the context of the act is not so often used.

This act was performed just before the Passover and soon before He was to leave His followers. It appears that the fact that the Father "had given all things into his hands, and that he was come from God, and went to God," was standing out in His mind in a special way—not that it was a new thought, but like a star made more brilliant by the crisp atmosphere of a cloudless sky, it shone in greater luster.

A very important principle of the Christian life is illustrated here. It takes greatness to stoop to life's menial tasks. When one is certain of his palatial home on the hill with its viands, he is not embarrassed to eat in a hovel. It is the "near rich" that can't be caught with the poor. It is the holy who can sit by the harlot in safety, when the one who is not far removed from such a life should refrain from such closeness.

Here Jesus was illustrating a mark of greatness that He had been teaching. He had likened himself to the servant

12

from the field, serving his lord, and not as the one sitting at meat. He came to take life's lowest seat and to teach His followers to do the same.

Jesus said, "I have given you an example" (John 13:15); it was that, but it was more than an example that should mold their lives—it was a pattern of the life that He always followed while on earth.

The blessing that should come from such a way of life would come from the doing: "Happy are ye if ye do them" (John 13:17). It is not enough to subscribe to the principle; it is the practice that gives the light. The Lord found the Pharisees teaching many good things, but of them He said, "They say, and do not" (Matt. 23:3). The "do not" canceled out the "say."

On another occasion, He asked, "Why call ye me, Lord, Lord, and do not the things which I say?" (Luke 6:46). Christian words, to be effective, must be backed up with Christian acts.

By this act we are taught that humility is an act of greatness. To stoop is a proof of superiority. Jesus did not deny His superior status: "Ye call me Master and Lord: and ye say well; for so I am" (John 13:13). He could not be true and deny that, for He was the only begotten Son of God, but He was saying, My stooping is the proof of My stature; My service gives testimony to My greatness. I rule from the servant's seat. My usefulness is in My giving, and not in receiving.

The true follower of Christ is a servant. He seeks to do for others and not to have them do for him. He is willing to pour out because he knows that he has "in heaven a better and an enduring substance" (Heb. 10:34).

One who has no certainty of riches in heaven is loathe to turn loose of what he has on earth, while the Christians to whom the Hebrew letter was addressed "took joyfully the spoiling of [their] goods," because they had better in heaven.

It was this very consciousness of Christ's connection

13

with the Father and His soon going to Him that made foot washing a pleasant chore. He could afford it. He had a high seat and crown awaiting Him.

Those who are not sure of a crown in the heavens seek all the honors of time that they can get, while those who are sure of heavenly honors can "in honour [prefer] one another" (Rom. 12:10).

It was the certainty of that "city which hath foundations, whose builder and maker is God" (Heb. 11:10) that caused Abraham to allow Lot to take the choice land of Palestine. He had better.

One does not mind giving away the extra suit in his bag if he has 10 good ones back at home. The one with no extra must fight to hold his own.

The blindness of Peter in refusing the Master's act of service but illustrates the almost universal blindness of people to the true meaning of Christianity. "Know ye what I have done to you?" (John 13:12). This question, addressed to the disciples, is a question made necessary today.

Do the followers of the Master know what Jesus was doing, and can they act with the same personal knowledge? He knew that He had come from God and was going back to God. Do we know that? Where did we come from if not from God? We were made in His image—we came from His heart and, like Jesus, are going back to Him. In such consciousness, we can afford to turn the other cheek, seek not our own, and suffer gladly for Christ's sake.

The perennial problem seems to be that gilded toys of time are so attractive that we fail to see the enduring treasure, and the plaudits of men overshadow the praise of God. Time seems to hold us in its orbit, while the heavenly seems so remote.

Jesus seemed to live in the consciousness of the heavenly all the time. He cultivated the contacts with His Father. He withdrew from the clanking coins of Caesar to note the trea-

14

sures of the skies. In so doing, He marked the path for us. "Follow me" is His call to all, and a call to follow Him in the consciousness of heavenly reward as well as of humble service.

We need not be in the dark as to how such living paid off. The story is clearly told: "Wherefore God also hath highly exalted him, and given him a name which is above every name" (Phil. 2:9).

The eternal wealth of Jesus is not for himself alone. He proposes to share it all with His own. We are declared to be "heirs of God, and joint-heirs with Christ" (Rom. 8:17). All that is His, is His to be shared. He lived not for self in time and will be living for others in eternity. He will share. He can afford to, for, as He declared, "All things that the Father hath are mine" (John 16:15). They can never be exhausted, so to share them will be eternal joy.

With a keen sense of the assurance of a God connection, we can go out to exemplify the Master's teaching and His example. Then will we understand the happiness of doing.

What Hath God Wrought!

The words "What hath God wrought!" spoken by the ancient seer, Balaam, when he viewed the Israelites en route to the Promised Land (Num. 23:23), are said to be the first message to cross the Atlantic cable.

In the truest sense the laying of the Atlantic cable was a work of man and not God. Such a feat could be, and probably was, carried out by men who had no fear of God. God does provide strength and resources for all of man's endeavors whether he uses them for God's glory or not, but they are the "works of men's hands" and not of the hand of God.

There is, however, a work wrought of God that He, and He alone, can do. It is the transformation of sinful men into saints fit for companionship with Him. Paul sets forth so graphically a picture of the raw material with which Christ begins His Church. He pictures the lowest, the vilest, and most undesirable of all creatures with which Christ builds His kingdom.

Let Paul give us the picture: "Be not deceived: neither fornicators, nor idolaters, nor adulterers, nor effeminate, nor abusers of themselves with mankind, nor thieves, nor covetous, nor drunkards, nor revilers, nor extortioners, shall inherit the kingdom of God" (1 Cor. 6:9-10).

Having listed those who would be shut out of the Kingdom, he writes to the group, "And such were some of you: but ye are washed, but ye are sanctified, but ye are justified in the name of the Lord Jesus, and by the Spirit of our God" (v. 11).

Here the lowest, the vilest, and the most undesirable have been cleansed, sanctified, and justified before God, and help to form the Bride of Christ. Here we can stand and proclaim in all sincerity, "What hath God wrought!" For He alone can do such things.

Here is a picture of redeeming grace, transforming the filth of the gutter into "saints in light" (Col. 1:12). Should we be tempted to despise those who have been thus redeemed, the Voice from above speaking to Peter should halt us: "What God hath cleansed, that call not thou common" (Acts 10:15).

This lesson sparkles with truths we should never forget. It shows us that the grace of God can reach the lowest, cleanse the vilest, and make them companions of Christ. It would teach us also that in God's sight (and it should be in ours) the vile sins of the past are gone, and the sinner has been made holy.

It tells us also that God can work where man cannot work, and do that which only He can do. It tells us also that the apostle had no sense of shame in associating with these holy people who were once vile and unlovable.

It teaches us also that we should never despair of our sinning friends and neighbors. God's transforming power is available to them all and is within reach of all.

It teaches us also that the true Church accepts on equal status those who have fallen low and those like the rich young ruler who can claim, "All these have I kept from my youth up" (Luke 18:21 et al.).

It tells us that our position in God's kingdom does not rest upon our past, be it clean or vile, but upon our present standing with Him.

It teaches us that in redemptive work we must depend upon and expect the miraculous. We should never despair but always have faith in a Father's love.

It teaches us also that only by the presence of lives transformed can the power of God be revealed. The change is the proof—the change that man has so often attempted and never accomplished; the change that is sudden and complete; the change as great as the change from death to life. Such is the change that reveals God.

One of the great hindrances in our day to the progress of salvation is the scarcity of such divinely wrought changes. Too often, the change has been made by the work of man's own hands and attributed to God. It is not convincing, and the gospel loses its proof. The changed life has always been a successful witness.

The dead man—"dead in trespasses and sins" (Eph. 2:1)—standing alive among the living cannot be spoken against. When God moves in His own power, He must be accounted with.

"What hath God wrought!" He has cleansed the sin-stained soul and made it meet for His indwelling. He has taken the discarded fibers of a worthless life and woven them into sinews of moral strength. He has made the sin-crippled soul to leap at the music of the heavenly chorus. He hath wrought wonders in gutters, in the slime pits, in the cesspools of moral shame. He has transformed the spineless into pillars of strength. He has taken the ignorant and given them wisdom unknown to mere human thought.

He stands among us to do His work today as He has done it in ages past. He is looking for helpers, those who believe that He can do the impossible and accomplish all that He attempts if He can but get the cooperation that He requires. His working has been through men; His limitations have been in His helpers and not in His help.

If Paul could say to the Corinthians, "Ye are not straitened in us, but ye are straitened in your own bowels" (2 Cor. 6:12), how much more can God say that He is limited by His "O ye of little faith" disciples (Matt. 6:30; Luke 12:28).

God can do a work beyond our comprehension! It is for us to believe and witness and work accordingly.

The Driver and the Steering Wheel

The value of a steering wheel is in proportion to its response to the hands of the driver. Given a perfect driver, any movement of the wheel contrary to the hand of the driver could be dangerous or even fatal. The total amenability of the wheel to the driver's hand illustrates the kind of total commitment of a life to God. This is the ideal.

Was there ever such a life lived? Was such an ideal ever reached? Was there ever a life whose every movement was directed by another? The answer is yes, but only one. The only begotten Son, and He alone, could say, "I do always those things that please him" (John 8:29), and have that testimony verified from above, "This is my beloved Son, in whom I am well pleased" (Matt. 3:17).

The Father was at the wheel of the Son's life, and the wheel was in perfect submission to the Father's hand; therefore, the acts of Christ were the acts of God, and the words of Christ were the words of God. These facts Jesus affirmed: "The word which ye hear is not mine, but the Father's which sent me" (John 14:24), and "The Father that dwelleth in me, he doeth the works" (v. 10).

The people of His day heard His words and saw His acts; they saw the wheel turning here and there, but He denied that He was doing the steering. The visible life that He lived was lived by an invisible Other. Of no other can this be said, but it can be said of the perfect Son of God.

19

While this ideal will never be reached by mortal men, our lives are valuable and pleasing to the Father as we approach thereto; therefore, our being pleasing in His sight is a relative thing and not an absolute one. The continuous chastening of the Lord is an ever-present reminder that the perfect has not been reached. And although one may testify with one of old, "I . . . have not wickedly departed from my God" (2 Sam. 22:22), he must confess that his walk is not perfect and that he often lags far behind in his attempt to follow.

For those who desire to walk more closely, these suggestions are offered:

First: There must be purposeful commitment to the Hand at the wheel. There can be no reservation in this purpose to yield; at times yielding may be hard or hesitant, but it must be purposed.

Second: There must be an ever-growing acquaintance with the Driver. One must learn to think as He thinks, ascertain the goals to which He is taking us and the paths by which the journey is to be made.

Time is required here, for no acquaintance can be gained instantly; an introduction, yes, but acquaintance, no. An ancient traveler advised, "Acquaint now thyself with him, and be at peace" (Job 22:21). This is good advice, for no one can have peace without knowing the Director of life.

Peace comes by knowing God, knowing that He understands us, that He always provides the best for His children, that He will never leave us, and that we are secure in Him and need have no anxious care.

To maintain this peace growing out of intimate acquaintance, a never-ending study of His Word must be maintained. Here we have a story of how He has dealt with His children in days past; and since He never changes, we may rest assured that He will care for us too.

Third: There must be an immediate response to His will. Jesus said, "I must work the works of him that sent me, while it is day" (John 9:4). He had no desired end to reach, no message to deliver, and no duty to perform that lay outside His Father's will. It is for us to practice this same pattern of living, which means that one must keep in touch with the Director and ever be at the work He has assigned.

At this point, distinction should be made between the assignments of God and those of others. Our amenability is to be to One and to those under whose care He has placed us.

Fourth: There must be the assurance that one will not be cut off if he comes short of the ideal. Even if sin should invade one's soul, there is forgiveness by the Advocate, who ever works toward the end of reconciliation.

Fifth: There must be complete trust that direction will be given. We must seek it in faith, nothing wavering, lest we get nothing because of our doubts. There must also be confidence that if we seek first the kingdom of God and His righteousness that all these things will be added.

Sixth: The knowledge gained by constant fellowship with the Director must not be hidden like a candle under a bushel but must be shared with others—not grudgingly or of constraint but through compassion and love, desiring for them the benefits that we have received.

Seventh: Last, but by no means least, there must be a passionate desire to press on to perfection, saying with Paul, "Not as though I had already attained . . . but I follow after" (Phil. 3:12).

The motivation of such ardent desire and tireless effort must be the desire to be like Him who was perfect. Christlikeness is ever the goal of our seeking, and a place by Him in the eternities ahead, our most coveted prize.

The desire to please the Father must be paramount. To this end "Christ pleased not himself" (Rom. 15:3), and to be like Him, to please the Father must be our highest pleasure.

The likeness of the Father is thus sought because there can be nothing higher in time or eternity. This is life's greatest goal, and all one's strength should be exercised toward its attainment.

The most glorious thing about the whole matter is the assurance that our search, although incompletely rewarded in time, will be fully rewarded in the life to come, for "we shall be like him; [when] we shall see him as he is" (1 John 3:2).

Our imperfect seeking will be rewarded by a perfect finding. Such is the grace of our Lord. He does not demand the absolute here. He bears with our feeble and, at times, grumbling efforts, and although we are like "smoking flax," He will not quench us (Matt. 12:20).

With such assurance we brave the tests and temptations and keep stumbling along—at times "cast down, but not destroyed" (2 Cor. 4:9), yet ever pressing onward, knowing that "faithful is he that calleth you, who also will do it" (1 Thess. 5:24).

They Were Sore Afraid

Man has always been fearful of beings from another realm; whether real or imaginary, they have produced fear. Spooks, ghosts, or angels have been objects of fear.

When messengers from heaven have made their appearance, men have grown fearful. This is almost universally true.

When God came to the Garden of Eden, Adam "was afraid." When Sarah heard the message of the angels, "she was afraid" (Gen. 3:10; 18:15). When "God called unto [Moses] out of the midst of the bush, . . . Moses hid his face; for he was afraid to look upon God" (Exod. 3:4, 6). Moses and Aaron often "fell upon their faces" when God came to them.

When Samuel appeared unto Saul after Samuel's death, "Saul fell straightway all along on the earth, and was sore afraid" (1 Sam. 28:20).

When God stretched forth His hand to protect the ark, "David was afraid of the Lord that day" (2 Sam. 6:9). When an angel came to destroy the inhabitants of Jerusalem, "David could not go before [the tabernacle] to enquire of God: for he was afraid" (1 Chron. 21:30).

When God began to make revelations to Ezekiel, the prophet "fell upon his face"; again and again it is written that "he fell upon his face" when God began to speak.

When the angel came near to Daniel, he said, "I was afraid, and fell upon my face" (Dan. 8:17). When a vision came to him, he said, "I have retained no strength . . . I became dumb" (10:16, 15).

Micah tells us that "the nations . . . shall be afraid of the Lord our God" (7:16-17).

Habakkuk tells us that he said, "O Lord, I have heard thy speech, and was afraid" (3:2).

When Zacharias saw the angel, "he was troubled, and fear fell upon him" (Luke 1:12). The shepherds were "sore afraid" when the angel came (2:9).

When Jesus appeared on the sea, the disciples were afraid.

When the Voice from above spoke to Jesus on the Mount of Transfiguration, the disciples were "sore afraid" (Matt. 17:6; Mark 9:6).

When angels were seen at Jesus' tomb, the women "were afraid" (Luke 24:5). Also, the angel in Cornelius' home caused him to fear.

Saul fell in fear when Christ appeared to him on the road to Damascus.

Twice the sainted John fell at the angel's feet.

From the beginning of time to the last recorded appearances of messengers from another world, men have been afraid. The very fact of someone from an unknown world is uncanny, frightening.

This same somewhat fear-provoking feeling comes to the Christian when the Spirit begins to speak to his heart. It is strange and at times unbelievable. The question persists, Is this God or not?

The question, at times, is further accentuated by the fact that the message seems to be so unbelievable. Like the promise to Abraham of a son, it seems so impossible. The first impression may be to forget it, or it may be to accept without question, and believe, and be disappointed. The enemy uses both methods. He takes the course most likely to accomplish his will.

Shock, uncertainty, distress, and fear are normal reactions to the appearances of God in our lives. Just as the visible appearances of old perturbed the saint, so do now the inner, invisible revelations.

When Jesus appeared as a ghost, walking on the sea, and the disciples cried out in fear, He quieted them with "Be of good cheer; it is I; be not afraid" (Matt. 14:27).

This same quieting Voice will always be heard if it is the Master approaching. At the beginning there may be uncertainty, even fear, but in the end, peace and quiet.

The beautiful thing about following Christ is that He demands or desires no action from us until His identity has become clear. We do not need to try to make His manifestation clear; that is His prerogative.

Give Him time and all will be plain, and nothing should be done until it is. One need not pour water on the fleece; we may lay out the fleece, but if we water it, we but deceive ourselves. That is His task, and He is well able to perform it.

The act of identifying the speaker is one that must be learned by the beginner, the one who seeks to follow a Person and will not be satisfied to follow a program. And too much emphasis cannot be placed upon the necessity of being calm. "I will give you rest" (Matt. 11:28). This is Christlikeness. There need be no bluster and rush, no fearing of missing the plane. Just keep with the Pilot.

This matter of conversing with One from another world—this ability to discern good from evil, self from Satan, and Satan from God—does not come in an instantaneous work of grace. It is a mark of maturity. It comes "by reason of use" (Heb. 5:12-14).

At the burning bush, Moses "hid his face; for he was afraid to look upon God" (Exod. 3:6). But after a lifetime of visits with God, long interviews, testing His messages, seeking His guidance, obeying His commands, it is written of him, "My servant Moses . . . is faithful . . . With him will I speak mouth to mouth" (Num. 12:7-8). "And the Lord spake unto Moses face to face, as a man speaketh unto his friend" (Exod.

33:11). "And there arose not a prophet since in Israel like unto Moses, whom the Lord knew face to face" (Deut. 34:10).

The secret of Moses' intimacy with God is stated thus: "Moses was faithful in all his house" (Heb. 3:2).

"God is no respecter of persons" (Acts 10:34). The promise still is given, recorded in John 14:21: "I will . . . manifest myself to him." The conditions of such manifestation are clearly set forth, and the door to His heart is wide open.

"Come unto me" is the universal invitation in Matt. 11:28, and our response should be, "Let us therefore come boldly unto the throne of grace" (Heb. 4:16).

In His last great prayer, Jesus asked for this oneness with His own—intimacy such as He had with the Father. His heart yearns for us, and when we desire it more than silver or gold, we can enter in. I am doing better and reaching forth for more!

Be Ye Followers of Me

(1 Cor. 4:16)

Paul, in one of his boldest statements, requested the Corinthian church, "Be ye followers of me." He spoke in qualified terms to the same church, "Be ye followers of me, even as I also am of Christ" (11:1). He wrote the church at Philippi in the same vein: "Brethren, be followers together of me, and mark them which walk so as ye have us for an ensample" (3:17). He seemed to rejoice that the church at Thessalonica followed him: "Ye became followers of us, and of the Lord" (1 Thess. 1:6). Later he reminded the same church: "Yourselves know how ye ought to follow us" (2 Thess. 3:7).

Paul definitely held himself up as an example. He believed in himself and his salvation. He had touched Christ and was assured of Him. He could recommend his pattern of life, for it led to peace, so he wrote, "Those things, which ye have both learned, and received, and heard, and seen in me, do: and the God of peace shall be with you" (Phil. 4:9).

One should live in such a manner that he can say to all, "Do as I do." This is God's plan; He expects it. Our Lord condemned the Pharisees: "They say, and do not" (Matt. 23:3).

We are commanded, "Be thou an example of the believers, in word, in conversation, in charity, in spirit, in faith, in purity" (1 Tim. 4:12). This is the commandment, and is it a sin to say that we are keeping it (that is, if we are)? I am persuaded that the main reason why so many will not say, "Follow me," is not because of their humility, but because they secretly know that they are living beneath the commandments of God.

Paul was so sure of his relationship with God and was so satisfied with that relationship that he wanted everyone to be like himself. He said to a king, "I would to God, that not only thou, but also all that hear me this day, were both almost, and altogether such as I am, except these bonds" (Acts 26:29).

Paul was a great salesman because he believed in his product. He had cast in his all to find Christ and counted the price as dung. He was satisfied.

In contrast, I meet so many professed Christians who have taken it up only to escape hell. They don't enjoy it, and they create no desire in anyone else for it. Could it be said that such are Christians? God knows, I don't; I will leave them with Him. I can say they are poor salesmen.

Why should one hesitate to say, "Follow me"? If he had been thirsty all day and had found a bubbling spring, would he not call his thirsty mates to come? The almost unanswerable argument is that if one is not a witness, he has not found satisfaction himself. "We cannot but speak the things which we have seen and heard" (Acts 4:20). That is real witnessing. It is not the water that is pumped, but that from Christ's "well of water springing up into everlasting life" (John 4:14). Rivers, flowing rivers is the promise; not seepage from the muck-filled branch, but rivers—rivers wide enough that one cannot swim across. This is the way of life that is telling.

To be able and willing to join the apostle Paul in saying, "Follow me," one must have some definite assurances. He must know that the Spirit of the living God has made His home in his heart. He must have the witness of the Spirit himself bearing witness with his spirit that he belongs to God and that God is within reigning.

He must have found that which is more precious to him than anything that the world can offer. His devotion to God must be so deep that no voice from a different source can allure him away. He must count "all things but loss" for Christ (Phil. 3:8).

To seek that others follow, he must be able to announce victory over all sin and assurance of God's keeping power in every emergency of life. He must have tested the goodness, the power, and the presence of the Holy Spirit, and found Him to be fully satisfying.

He must be sure "that if our earthly house of this tabernacle were dissolved, we have a building of God . . . not made with hands, eternal in the heavens" (2 Cor. 5:1). He must fully believe in the resurrection of the dead and the rewards of the saints. In short, he must be fully persuaded that he is on the winning side.

To invite others to follow, one must have experienced enough of God's grace as to be persuaded, fully persuaded, that "he is able to keep that which I have committed unto him against that day" (2 Tim. 1:12).

To ask for followers is to see the way through, and more than that, to know that Christ is along. Paul could say, "Follow me," for Christ was by his side, and to follow Paul was to be in company with Christ. He was not alone, and the invitation to follow was an invitation to Christ. In fact, Paul was but extending the invitation for Christ's sake. To be with Paul was to be with Christ.

When our assurance of the conscious presence of the Spirit, purifying our souls and possessing our lives, has become a consuming passion, our desire for others to be with us will be apparent.

It was not egotism, boasting, or vanity that made Paul call for followers; the very love of Christ was constraining. He burned with love and zeal; he had found the pearl of great price—the way to eternal life—and he called upon all to join him.

He wanted all to be saved, happy, and secure, and there

was only one way to reach it. He had found it, so he said, "Follow me." To go any other way would be to miss it.

With such assurance, drive, and love, someone will follow. Our appeal is for us to be so sure of ourselves that we can urge all to become like us, followers of Christ. Fire is catching, ice is not. May the fires of dedication, satisfaction, and love burn so brightly and so hot that God will be glorified in our midst.

I Have No Desire to Be an Original Thinker

Many times I have heard people sing the praises of one whom they called "an original thinker." Whatever an original thinker may be, I have no desire to be one, for I do not find this desire in either Christ or the Holy Spirit. My deepest desire is to be able, in a limited measure, to think the thoughts of God after Him; this was the desire of both Jesus and the Holy Spirit.

Jesus claimed to speak only what He had been taught: "As my Father hath taught me, I speak these things" (John 8:28). His judgments were limited to what He heard: "As I hear, I judge" (5:30). Again, "I speak to the world those things which I have heard of him" (8:26).

When the Holy Spirit came, He was content to be an echo; He had no yen to be original. Of Him it was said, "He shall not speak of himself; but whatsoever he shall hear, that shall he speak" (John 16:13).

God provides the same Instructor for us that Christ and the Holy Spirit had and used. "It is written in the prophets, And they shall be all taught of God" (John 6:45). Why then should we seek to go out on our own?

Man's highest privilege in the field of thought is to be able to think the thoughts of God after Him. What could be higher than to think His thinking, to revel in what He knows?

Intellectual pride is dealt a deadly blow when one renounces his own originality and seeks only to listen and to copy, to think along the trails of the divine thinking, and echo those thoughts upon earth. Should one aspire to such a pattern of thought, what prerequisites must be met to enable him thus to think?

First: He must be childlike, unassuming, receptive, trustful, and meek. The arrogance of the learned must be supplanted by the humility of the unspoiled child. The quiet meekness of the Master must pervade the soul. Argumentativeness must bow in humility and the mind be washed clean for the divine imprint.

Second: The mind must be attuned to the heavenly and divorced from the worldly—although in the world, yet not of it. The affections must pull the mind to the imperishable, and one's entire journey must be as that of a pilgrim looking for a permanent residence.

Third: One must remember that God's thoughts are not as our thoughts, and our thinking His thoughts after Him will be out of line with the thinking of the world. This basic difference must be accepted if one is to enter into the mind of God. The Word clearly teaches that the spiritual cannot be understood by the nonspiritual, and godlikeness itself puts a barrier between the citizen and the pilgrim. To be at home here is to be unprepared for the heavenly hereafter. The Christian who walks close to the Master groans within himself, awaiting the hour of his deliverance.

Fourth: The thinking of His thoughts can come only when the thinking of men has lost its magic appeal. So long as the glamour of worldly wisdom enthralls the mind, the wisdom of God remains unsought. The power that opens the eye of the soul to the one at the same time closes the eye of the soul to the other. They are mutually exclusive of each other.

Fifth: One must have due appreciation for the heavenly wisdom. This evaluation must be more than a profession; it must be a possession, and if a possession, it will bear the marks of it. Some indications of its presence are:

1. An ardent desire for divine wisdom

   a. "Blessed are they which do hunger and thirst after righteousness" (Matt. 5:6).

   b. "I rejoice at thy word, as one that findeth great spoil" (Ps. 119:162).

   c. "Mine eyes prevent the night watches, that I might meditate in thy word" (Ps. 119:148).

2. A willingness to devote time to obtain it

   a. "Yea, if thou criest after knowledge, and liftest up thy voice for understanding . . . then shalt thou understand" (Prov. 2:3, 5).

   b. "I opened my mouth, and panted: for I longed for thy commandments" (Ps. 119:131).

   c. Christ spent long hours in the school of the Father.

Sixth: One must have a precommitment to his findings: "If any man will do his will, he shall know" (John 7:17). This total precommitment to the whole known and unknown will of God is indispensable if one is to participate in His thoughts.

Seventh: He must have faith that the searching will not be in vain. Finding has been promised, and the seeker must expect to be taken into the thought and the mind of the Great Teacher by the guidance of the Holy Spirit. "The meek will he guide" is a promise that will not be broken (Ps. 25:9).

If this pattern of thought appears to be a narrow one, the answer is, "It is." Like the way to eternal life, it is narrow. It skirts all the bypaths and holds tenaciously to the narrow way.

While the way that leads to life is narrow, life itself is broad, high, wide, and endless. To enter into the thinking of the Highest is to be introduced to the mysteries of the Kingdom, open only to the ardent seeker. It is to see light in His light. It is to reevaluate all things temporal and tag the eternal as priceless, and the temporal as of little worth.

When the true values have been placed on each item, the things eternal become all-important. One begins to understand the words of the Master, "What is a man profited, if he shall gain the whole world, and lose his own soul?" (Matt. 16:26). The thoughts of the soul now leap to the paths of the divine thinking, and the whole life begins to be molded into the pattern of the divine. The rules of the heavenly now become the laws to guide our mortal lives. We think with God on the conduct of the soul. The Sermon on the Mount becomes the pattern of our life, and the Golden Rule our yardstick of action.

More and more our thoughts, actions, and spirit become molded into the pattern of the Master as the mind of God is allowed to permeate our being. One ceases to hew out a kingdom for himself, and strives to bring in the kingdom of God. His mind now runs in the channels of the spiritual, and much of what he once considered necessary becomes secondary, or even worthless.

His mind reaches ever upward to grasp the thoughts of the Highest, and pouring it through the channel of his own thinking, brings God's thoughts down to men. The mind of man has been exchanged for the mind of the Master. What greater privilege is there than to be able to think the thoughts of God after Him!

God Hath Chosen the Poor—the Rich

James calls upon the "beloved brethren" to "hearken," for he was about to impart a very important truth. He was to tell them who God had chosen to be "heirs of the kingdom." The truth was to be a shocking one to some of them, for the heirs were to be those who were "the poor of this world."

This appears to be a strange choice on the part of God, but when God chooses, there is a reason for the choice. He charges, "Ye have despised the poor," and yet these very despised poor are to be chosen as heirs of the Kingdom (2:5-6).

Why bypass the rich, or at least choose so few of that class? The answer to this question is written in many places in the Word.

"How hardly shall they that have riches enter into the kingdom of God!" (Mark 10:23; Luke 18:24) was an issue raised by Jesus often in His ministry. He warned of the "deceitfulness of riches [that] choke the word" (Matt. 13:22; Mark 4:19).

Money can buy so many things that one desires, things needful and legitimate. But alas! it can also buy that which is illegitimate. The juror has been known to cast an unjust vote for a fee; judges have rendered verdicts for a price; widows and orphans have been robbed for illicit gain; and a multitude of crimes are committed for money's sake.

Since money can do so many things and get so much, it is difficult to have it and not rely upon it. Jesus saw this and exclaimed, "How hard is it for them that trust in riches to enter into the kingdom of God!" (Mark 10:24).

So deceitful and dangerous are riches that when the Son of Man was made "in fashion as a man" (Phil. 2:8), He stripped himself of all wealth. "Ye know the grace of our Lord Jesus Christ, that, though he was rich, yet for your sakes he became poor" (2 Cor. 8:9). He did not propose to have His own soul influenced by wealth, nor the success of His ministry attributed to His financial standing.

The baneful effects of riches are pointed out to us in various places in the Word. The rich young ruler went away "very sorrowful" (Luke 18:23-24); he had too much to give up. Paul reminded Timothy that "they that will be rich fall into temptation and a snare, and into many foolish and hurtful lusts, which drown men in destruction and perdition" (1 Tim. 6:9), and warned this young minister to "flee these things"—not *to* them (as seems to be the present-day practice), but to flee *from* them (v. 11).

James reminds his hearers that riches tend to make their owners despise the poor and then to "oppress" them (2:6).

The Revelator tells us our Lord's words that riches tend to make one blind and boastful: "Thou sayest, I am rich . . . and have need of nothing; and knowest not that thou art wretched, and miserable, and poor, and blind, and naked" (Rev. 3:17).

James depicts the closing days of rich men: "Go to now, ye rich men, weep and howl for your miseries that shall come upon you. Your riches are corrupted . . . Your gold and silver is cankered; [they] shall eat your flesh as it were fire" (James 5:1-3).

For these and other reasons, God has chosen the poor. "Blessed be ye poor: for yours is the kingdom of God. . . . But woe unto you that are rich! for ye have received your consolation" (Luke 6:20, 24). "Let not the rich man glory in his riches" (Jer. 9:23) is the command; but since that is so easy to do, God has bypassed the group that thus glories and chooses those whose glory is not in things, "that no flesh should glory in his presence" (1 Cor. 1:29).

If we should close our message here, the poor of the whole world—good, bad, and even wicked—would begin to rejoice in their poverty and feel assured of a place in the coming Kingdom; but James was not talking of all the poor; he was speaking of the class from which the calling would be made. But few of the poor in this world's goods will enter the kingdom. James limits the group to those poor who are "rich in faith." That leaves most of the poor out, for "broad is the way, that leadeth to destruction, and many there be which go in thereat" (Matt. 7:13).

Only the poor who are "rich in faith" can enter the Kingdom. This richness of faith must have a beginning, for "without faith it is impossible to please him" (Heb. 11:6). Poverty does not please Him, but the faith of the poor does. This required faith leads to the new birth, for "ye must be born again" (John 3:7). This necessary faith leads also to holiness, "without which no man shall see the Lord" (Heb. 12:14).

This rich faith that is required for Kingdom entrance is one that seeks first the kingdom of God and His righteousness. It lays up its treasures in heaven. It loves not the world nor the things in the world. The emoluments of wealth and the plaudits of men have been sacrificed on the altar of a total dedication to God. "They are not of the world, even as I am not of the world," Christ said (John 17:16).

They have forsaken all to follow the poor Man from Nazareth. They count not their lives dear unto themselves. For Him they have suffered the loss of all things and count that which was thus lost as dung. They have become "strangers and pilgrims" here "on the earth," and "God is not ashamed" to call them brethren but has "prepared for them a city" (Heb. 11:13, 16)—the city that John saw coming down.

These are the "poor . . . rich in faith" that God has chosen. They were chosen, not because they were poor, but in spite of their poverty; they were chosen because they were "rich in faith"—faith that if they would die with Him, they would live with Him; faith that if they would humble themselves, He would exalt them; faith that if their treasures were laid up in heaven, that moth and rust could not corrupt them and thieves could not break in and steal.

The poor with such richness of faith are the chosen for the Kingdom. Such faith is open to all, but the poor grasp it more easily than the rich; hence, "Blessed be ye poor" (Luke 6:20). They begin with no financial hindrances or handicaps.

Set Your Affection on Things

God has made us to enjoy things. True, our first and major love is for personalities. We are to love God with all our heart, and then our neighbor as ourselves. Having met the major requirement of love, we then give ourselves to the minor duty—the love of things.

We cannot divorce ourselves from things, neither in this life nor in the life to come. Things were made for man. In the very beginning, God made things for His only Son. "All things were created . . . for him . . . visible and invisible . . . that are in heaven, and that are in earth" (Col. 1:16). So there are visible things in heaven as well as in earth, and we are commanded to set our affection on things.

From a very casual observation it would appear that man needs but little exhortation at this point. Things seem to be major in the conversation of most people with whom I associate. In a typical visit in the home of friends, the conversation runs almost fully to things. The talk is of the new car, the furniture recently refinished, the antique piece that was picked up while scouring a remote mountainous region, the fishing trip, the new school building, the income tax, the anticipated job—in short, the materialities of life. Things seem to have almost completely filled the horizon of thought and speech.

It is a rare thing to find one who has but little interest in things. The commandment to set your affection on things seems to be well followed. Things seem to hold the center. If this be true, why then the complaint? The problem? The affections are set on the wrong class of things. They are the things that perish.

There is another commandment that seeks to govern our love for such things. It runs thus: "Love not the world, neither the things that are in the world" (1 John 2:15).

To reinforce this command, it is written, "Set your affection on things above, not on things on the earth" (Col. 3:2). So it is not the love of things that is forbidden, but the love of the wrong things. It is the problem of misplaced love, and that is a part of man's basic problem—the misuse of the good.

The Word of God is replete with allusions to things—material things—in the heavens. Jesus exhorts us to live, serve, give, and suffer in such a way that we may have "treasures" in heaven. To one faithful man He said, "Have thou authority over ten cities" (Luke 19:17). To another He assigned five cities. We read of a river, fruit, harps, crowns, thrones, a new earth, and so on. Heaven abounds in "mansions" and other valuable things, and we are commanded to set our affection on these imperishable things.

There are innumerable benefits in following this advice.

First: It saves one from many of the keen disappointments that men otherwise have when the things of time crumble in their hands. The ill effect of temporal losses is determined largely by the extent to which our heart is entwined about them. To have one's affections set on things above saves one from the sorrow of temporal losses, at least from unbearable grief.

Second: It preserves all that matters most to the soul. When the love is for the things in the heavens, it is so placed that one cannot be disappointed. Thieves cannot break through and steal as in time, and moth and rust cannot corrupt. There can be no permanent loss of heavenly treasures.

Third: It guarantees God's help while we are here on earth. If we seek first the Kingdom, He has promised to add what He deems necessary.

Fourth: It brings permanent satisfaction to the soul. There is nothing of value in the passing things of time to meet the deep need of the soul of man. We are made primarily for eternity and not for time, and only eternal values can satisfy for long.

In my current rereading of Mr. Wesley's Journal I was impressed by his oft-repeated comment as to the transitoriness of time and things of this life. He often mentions his frequent visits to the beauty spots made by men, and the ruins of the palaces of the great and the castles of the nobility. Most generally he concludes his comments with some reference to the vaporlike life that amassed such buildings, the dissipation of the fortunes that made their construction possible, the glory of their once-brilliant owners, or the very certainty of the passing of the earth and the stars above it. He was a man who thought in terms of the eternal, which made of him a better steward of the temporal. The temporal was viewed in the light of the heavenly, and used so as to gain a better reward in eternity.

Abraham was a character who moved through a long and useful life by the lure of the things in the heavens. Of him it was said, "He looked for a city which hath foundations, whose builder and maker is God" (Heb. 11:10). Because of his certainty of a heavenly city, he was willing to live the life of a pilgrim and stranger on earth. He realized that this life will soon pass away, and whatever inconvenience or privation must be endured in time will be but for a moment. He was not disappointed, for of him and others of like faith it is said: "God is not ashamed to be called their God: for he hath prepared for them a city" (v. 16).

Moses was moved in like manner. He forsook all the

wealth of a prosperous empire because "he had respect unto the recompence of the reward" (Heb. 11:26). It has been the lure of the divinely promised rewards that has kept the feet of the faithful pressing the path of obedience through storm, persecution, and even death. It was "for the joy that was set before him" (12:2) that enabled Christ to bear the ignominy, shame, and death that He endured. All of this adds poignancy to Paul's penetrating observation, "If in this life only we have hope in Christ, we are of all men most miserable" (1 Cor. 15:19). Many of the pieces of the jigsaw puzzle of life lie beyond the vale. Only the revelations of the next world can place life in its true perspective. In the meantime, we have the divine assurance that all will be well for His followers.

One should never forget that we are in a warfare in an enemy's territory, and the tide is running in favor of the temporal; only by the help of the Divine may we be able to cut across the ideals, dreams, aspirations, and examples of those of the world. The craft on which the men of the world are sailing is both ablaze and sinking. We are to "save [ourselves] from this untoward generation" (Acts 2:40).

Finally, man is made to love. The Christian life is not one of cramped restraint, but one of full expression. Love, to be normal, must be full and happy, unrestrained. One cannot love the perishing things without restraint and be happy. They will not bear the weight of the soul. On the other hand, one can let love loose to roam the hills of God in anticipation of the eternal inheritance of the soul's tomorrow. Revelry here finds its true fulfillment—the dream has content and value. The vision is unfading, its realization sure.

This is not the idle dreaming of those who fabricate their own vision that fades at the dawn of truth and reality, but the dream inspired by reality—reality that is fadeless and time-less, as timeless as the One who inspired it, and as real as the heavens themselves. It is but the echo of the heavenly reality—the foretoken of that which most surely will be.

Strange as it may appear, it is not the visible that is abiding but the invisible. It is the dreamed of that will last, for God is a God of the dream and the Guarantor of its fulfillment.

The apostle Paul saw things when he was lifted up into the third heaven—things so glorious and grand that he was not permitted to convey his findings to the other saints.

John, from his island dungeon, was given visions of things yet to be seen by the saints. He was convinced of the grandeur and glory of that which is yet to be seen and enjoyed. He drew a few of those pictures for us to view. Others were so shocking that he was denied the privilege of passing them on to us. He had no misgivings as to the reality of the things above. To him the tree of life and the river of life were real and grand. The angels that he saw and heard were real, and their harps of gold were as real as the beaten gold on the altar of the ancient Tabernacle. There was reality in the skies. Things of all kinds moved before him. He saw them in preview and longed for the time of their universal viewing. God meant it when He said, "Set your affection on things"— "things above." He has never fooled us and never will. "Things" will be there. Look for them. Love them. They are yours.

A Rebuff or a Challenge?

The amazement of those who witnessed the miracles of Jesus must have been ecstatic at times, and it is not strange that some who observed His wonder-working power would desire to know its secret and be able to exercise it themselves.

Following one of His most wonderful miracles, they said to Him, "What shall we do, that we might work the works of God?" (John 6:28). The answer of Jesus was simple and straightforward: "This is the work of God, that ye believe on him whom he hath sent" (v. 29).

Most of my Christian life I took this answer to be a kind of mild rebuke. I thought that Jesus was saying to them, Forget the miraculous deeds and save your souls by believing on Me as Savior—that is the work of God for you.

But was Jesus saying that? That He wanted them to accept Him as Savior is certain, but was His reply intended as a rebuff or a challenge? Evidently they, like myself, considered it a kindly rebuke, and here the interview ended.

From more mature thinking, I have come to believe that Jesus was challenging them to higher heights of Christian achievement; but like His angel of old, He would leave us unblessed unless a desperate Jacob cried out, "I will not let thee go, except thou bless me" (Gen. 32:26).

God does not reveal His deeper secrets nor impart His choice gifts to the casual seeker. The first knock of the neighbor seeking bread brought forth no favorable response, and the unjust judge ignored the casual asking of the importunate widow—but her prolonged importunate pleading won a response. "If thou seekest her as silver, and searchest

44

for her as for hid treasures" (Prov. 2:4) is the requirement for the successful finder.

Jesus' questioners were too casual, their desire to follow too shallow, their faith too weak.

God's seeming indifference, the necessity of perseverance, and the reward of faith are all illustrated in the story of Elijah and Elisha. Elisha desired a double portion of his master's spirit and was promised it on the condition that he would see Elijah when he was taken away. The reward was to be at the end of the journey, but three times the old prophet invited Elisha to remain behind; on each occasion the young prophet answered, "As the Lord liveth, and as thy soul liveth, I will not leave thee" (2 Kings 2:2, 4, 6). And leave he did not. His untiring pursuit reflected his capacity for the honor soon to be bestowed. To have failed to press his case would have disqualified him for the blessing.

The questioners of Jesus were willing to drop their search for His secret power at the slightest discouraging word.

The reply of Jesus was a challenge and not a rebuff. He used the same words later as a challenge to His disciples. "He that believeth on me, the works that I do shall he do also" (John 14:12). It is evident that these words were spoken as a challenge and not as a rebuff, and yet they are the same words as spoken before. The earlier group didn't grasp His meaning and went listlessly away. To them the message was empty, the answer veiled.

Here it becomes painfully necessary to ask, Has this last-mentioned message become as empty and unanswered to us as the first one was to those who raised their questions?

Answering my own question in all the honesty that I knowingly possess, I must say, These words of Christ—if I understand their meaning—are to me empty of meaning and void of fulfillment.

If He was not saying to men of faith that the works that He was doing upon earth—the miracles He performed—are

45

accomplishable by men of faith, then I do not know the meaning of words.

The promise is made to him "that believeth on me," and if to thus believe is not within the pale of the possible, then the Master's words are meaningless and empty; yea, worse than that, they are sheer mockery. Such a charge cannot be made justly against Him who taught us, "Use not vain repetitions" (Matt. 6:7).

If this challenging statement of Jesus cannot be deleted honestly from the Word nor its meaning other than is plainly stated, then the onus must fall upon men who are without faith—faith to do exploits. The almost universal absence of such faith does not negate the possibility of it, else Jesus' words are meaningless.

One need neither mark off this promise as being void when the Master made it nor because there is virtually no apparent realization of it among us. We affirm its truthfulness because it was spoken by Him who is the Truth. We acknowledge the lack of fulfillment, for that, too, was predicted by Christ. "When the Son of man cometh, shall he find faith on the earth?" (Luke 18:8) must have been spoken with a sigh.

In spite of the unbelief of our age, we owe it to God, ourselves, and this bewildered age to seriously ask, "Why have we no such faith?"

The disciples asked the Master an honest question, "Why could not we cast him out?" (Matt. 17:19; Mark 9:28). And Jesus gave an immediate answer. Will He deny us an answer if we ask honestly with due confession?

The reproduction of the deeds of Jesus in our day would challenge the world and be a means of quickening faith for salvation. This is true unless results accruing from such works in the past would no longer accrue.

Whatever our answer and attitude may be, we are on safe ground when we heed the injunction, "Examine yourselves, whether ye be in the faith" (2 Cor. 13:5).

Where Are the Mockers?

"They mocked him." These harsh and bitter words reflect the attitude of the men of Jesus' day toward the Son of Man.

The fact of the mockery is well established; in fact, it was foreseen and predicted by Jesus. On the road to Jerusalem, Jesus told His disciples that He would be betrayed and mocked. This had been foretold by the prophets; it was inevitable, the normal reaction of sinful men against one who is holy. Jesus, the embodiment of holiness, was to meet that reaction. "They mocked him."

The brilliance of His holiness evoked the depth of their scorn. The mockery was widespread and ruthless. The multitude mocked Him, the Jews mocked Him, and the soldiers mocked Him. The chief priests mocked Him, Herod mocked Him, and those passing by the Cross mocked Him. It was the eruption of sinful man's venom against a holy God. Incarnate goodness encountered incarnate evil, and bitter mockery ensued.

If mockery is the normal reaction of the evil against the good, we may expect to find it in other cases where there is a confrontation between the evil and the good. Let the record speak here.

We can see the mockery of the natural man against the spiritual as Ishmael, the son of the bondwoman, mocks Isaac, the son of promise (cf. Gen. 21:9).

Right on into King Zedekiah's day, God sent prophets to warn the people, "but they mocked the messengers of God" (2 Chron. 36:16).

When God commissioned Nehemiah to rebuild the

47

walls of Jerusalem, Sanballat "mocked the Jews" (Neh. 4:1).

The Psalmist recounts that "with hypocritical mockers in feasts, they gnashed upon me with their teeth" (Ps. 35:16).

When the writer of Hebrews recounts the trials of Old Testament saints, he records, "Others had trial of cruel mockings and scourgings" (11:36). Saints have had some rough times just because they were saints.

The mocking of the Christian did not cease with Old Testament history. It was present at Pentecost. The disciples shared it when "others mocking said, These men are full of new wine" (Acts 2:13).

The mocking continued as the gospel of the miraculous was preached. "When they heard of the resurrection of the dead, some mocked" (17:32).

Although our illustrations are of necessity drawn from the past, since they are from the Word, the same Word assures us that such mockery is not a thing of the past. Jude reminds us that it will be present at the end period: "The apostles of our Lord Jesus Christ . . . told you there should be mockers in the last time" (vv. 17-18).

Wherever the spiritual has been dominant, the mocking has been in evidence. When the light shines brightly, those who will not walk in it reject and fight it. So we may expect persecution, ridicule, and mockery when the undimmed light is shining.

"Where are the mockers?" is a pertinent question. If mocking comes when the light is shining brightly, we should take a look at our light. Is it under a bushel, or is it going out? Few Christians will question the fact that "iniquity [does] abound" and Jesus said that because of that, "the love of many shall wax cold" (Matt. 24:12). Has our love waxed cold? This state comes upon one like a creeping paralysis; hence the injunction to "examine [ourselves]" (2 Cor. 13:5), lest we have drifted from center.

The enmity of the world toward the holy has never changed, and it increases as holy people become more aggressive in propagating the gospel; therefore, the well-nigh absence of the mockery is noteworthy.

The tendency of professed Christians is to be content with the status quo. When all is quiet on the front, we tend to sit and enjoy the peace, the peace of stagnation and death.

The Church of Christ is militant, it is aggressive, it is disturbing, it is a divisive force in a world of complacency and sin. The belligerent reaction of sinners comes only when our lives, our ministry, our witness disturbs them. When we "cry aloud, spare not, lift up [our] voice like a trumpet, and shew [the] people their transgression" as we are commanded (Isa. 58:1), it is then that the cry comes "to the seers, See not; and to the prophets, Prophesy not unto us right things, speak unto us smooth things, prophesy deceits" (30:16).

Opposition to dynamic Christianity is inevitable. "If the world hate you, ye know that it hated me before it hated you" (John 15:18). This hatred is based upon Christlikeness, and if it never comes, we are not like Christ. "Yea, and all that will live godly in Christ Jesus shall suffer persecution" (2 Tim. 3:12). Note the "all." If we always escape it, we are not living "godly" in Christ Jesus. It is just that simple.

Satanic opposition is as certain as can be if one is actively and aggressively bearing down upon the kingdom of Satan. If the Christian has stacked his weapons and is resting easy, the devil will become rather silent; but if we are using "the weapons of our warfare" to pull down the strongholds of the devil (2 Cor. 10:3-4), look out! He will be after us with persecution, ridicule, and mockings.

By and large, the Church is too much asleep to be a disturbing force to the devil. "Awake thou that sleepest" (Eph. 5:14) was never a more appropriate cry than today. "The night cometh, when no man can work" (John 9:4).

"The Son of God goes forth to war / . . . Who follows in His train?" To thus follow is to suffer, and to suffer is to reign. Choose your path.

Keep Yourselves in the Love of God

(Jude 21)

The subject that we have chosen is a clear and positive command of God. The command to "keep yourselves in the love of God" comes with as much force as "Love not the world" or "Rejoice evermore" (1 John 2:15; 1 Thess. 5:16). God makes no demands of us that we cannot meet. What He requires of us He stands ready to empower us to do. This command is no exception to the rule.

Should one inquire just how this commandment can be fulfilled, the answer is forthcoming. There is One who set the example for us and marked the way for us to follow. Jesus kept himself in the love of God. He kept himself thus before His incarnation. In one of His greatest prayers, He said to the Father, "Thou lovedst me before the foundation of the world" (John 17:24).

He maintained this relationship throughout His earthly life and repeatedly affirmed it. Note His declarations:

"The Father loveth the Son, and sheweth him all things that himself doeth" (John 5:20).

Later in life He said, "Therefore doth my Father love me, because I lay down my life" (John 10:17).

Jesus expected the disciples to have the same love in their hearts from the Father as He had; He prayed, "I have declared unto them thy name ... that the love wherewith thou hast loved me may be in them" (John 17:26).

He expected them to maintain the same love relationship with the Father as He maintained, and both by His example and by His teaching He pointed the way.

He wanted the world to know that He loved the Father, and He proposed to reveal it in its most effective way. He had already shown His followers that maximum human love would lay down its life for a friend. He was to take a step that only He could take and reveal the depth of divine love in giving His life for us while we were yet sinners.

Jesus was speaking in the context of such death when He said, "But that the world may know that I love the Father; and as the Father gave me commandment, even so I do. Arise, let us go hence" (John 14:31). His going was toward the Cross in obedience to the Father, which was the highest manifestation of love possible and the most convincing.

Here Jesus opens to us the secret of His keeping in the Father's love. It was by obedience. He further clarifies it by saying, "I have kept my Father's commandments, and abide in his love" (John 15:10).

Since Jesus affirms that He kept in His Father's love by keeping His commandments, and since He had told us earlier that the Father loved Him before the foundation of the world, it is evident that He maintained that preincarnate love by obedience. The laws of God and the Kingdom are the same in heaven and on earth, and for that reason Jesus taught us to pray that we should bring our earthly actions in line with the laws of heaven.

The postincarnate existence of Jesus will evidently follow this same law of abiding in love by obedience. We know that in the eternities future Jesus will be subject to the Father, and it is reasonable to assume that He will be thus subject for the same reason that He obeyed upon earth—namely, that He might abide in the Father's love. We know that in the final

51

consummation of things, Christ will be subject unto the Father; that we are clearly told: "Then shall the Son also himself be subject unto him that put all things under him, that God may be all in all" (1 Cor. 15:28).

The path that Jesus trod is clearly marked. He himself marked it out thus, "Lo, I come (in the volume of the book it is written of me,) to do thy will, O God" (Heb. 10:7), and He said that He was able to abide in His Father's love by so doing. It was that simple—abiding by obeying.

Having set the pattern by word and by deed, Jesus declares that we can and should follow in the same path. His words are: "If ye keep my commandments, ye shall abide in my love; even as I have kept my Father's commandments, and abide in his love" (John 15:10).

At first sight, it might appear that Jesus is here merely holding up a privilege, but that is not the case. The commandment is to "keep yourselves in the love of God," and the demand for obedience is reiterated more often still. In fact, one cannot remain saved without obeying. Many verses could be quoted, but one will illustrate: "Why call ye me, Lord, Lord, and do not the things which I say?" (Luke 6:46).

The call to obey is written upon almost every page of the Word; and if obeyed, the commandment to abide in His love would be thereby fulfilled.

Once again Christ has shown us the pattern of life, life that comes by death. He was the "corn of wheat" that was to fall into the ground and die and then live forever in fruitfulness (John 12:24).

The end was not death but eternal glory. It is true that Jesus said, "Therefore doth my Father love me, because I lay down my life" (John 10:17). If the sentence ended there, life would go out into darkness, but it doesn't end there. It continues, "that I might take it again"; and what a taking it was! "Wherefore God also hath highly exalted him, and given him a name which is above every name" (Phil. 2:9). He is seated with the Father in His throne; angels bow now, and mankind will bow later; glory, honor, and majesty will be His forever. The "wherefore" of verse 9 gives the key. He went down as the way up.

The pattern has been set, the way marked, the end revealed. Now comes the call to follow. The path is unchanged, the reward guaranteed: "To him that overcometh will I grant to sit with me in my throne, even as I also overcame, and am set down with my Father in his throne" (Rev. 3:21).

The end is not yet, for "He that overcometh shall inherit all things; and I will be his God, and he shall be my son" (21:7); and the Son is the Heir of God and "joint-heir" with the "children of God" (Rom. 8:16-17). Could anything be better? This is worth dying for, and that is the price—death, the door to life. I enter!

He Doth Not Resist You

(James 5:6)

In the Sermon on the Mount, which worldlings have called "impractical idealism," Jesus taught, "That ye resist not evil." He amplified this principle by saying that "whosoever shall smite thee on thy right cheek, turn to him the other also." When one loses his coat in a lawsuit, he is to give his "cloak also." When compelled to go a mile, one should go two (Matt. 5:39-41).

In a similar vein did He teach a line of conduct diametrically opposed to the thinking and practice of the natural man. If such teaching were put into practice, it would be revolutionary.

The question arises, Would anyone take Him seriously enough to follow His teaching? Could one survive the results of such manner of living? It is interesting to know that some did. James tells the story. He gives the record of those from whom their just wages were withheld while the unjust employers "lived in pleasure on the earth, and [had] been wanton." They went so far as to condemn and kill the just. The significant thing is "the just . . . doth not resist" (5:4-6).

Here the "just" are following the Master's teaching, "Resist not evil." It is interesting, too, to note that they are commended for their obedience. They are enjoined to "be patient . . . unto the coming of the Lord" (v. 7). They are reminded also that "the husbandman waiteth for the precious fruit of the earth." They were not to "grudge" one another. They were further encouraged to pursue their course of nonresistance by the example of the "prophets . . . for an example of suffering affliction, and of patience."

Job is held up to illustrate suffering and patience and a demonstration of the "tender mercy" of the Lord. They were also reminded that "the husbandman waiteth . . . the coming of the Lord draweth nigh" (vv. 7-11).

The course of action outlined here is so foreign to the spirit of this age and so unrealistic that it would never be followed except one have faith in God that He would protect the one thus obeying Him.

James refers to the "precious fruit" for which God is waiting. What is the fruit for which God is looking? The concluding verses of the sermon in which this teaching is found gives us the answer. After having announced these revolutionary rules, Jesus said that those who practiced them built upon the rock, others built upon sand. The precious fruit for which He waits are those who love and trust Him enough to obey His commandments.

When giving these strange and unheard-of commands, Jesus assured us that the "Father knoweth" our needs. We need not worry about the morrow. It would care for itself. We are better than the fowls that the Father feeds. He clothes the grass and would clothe us.

Jesus touched the center of the matter when He said, "O ye of little faith" (Matt. 6:30). If one really believed that God knew our needs and cared for us and would care for us, he would not hesitate to follow the pattern of life outlined by the Master. Our disobedience is proof of our lack of faith—faith to believe that God is truthful.

That we lack such faith is reflected in other areas of our lives. Jesus affirmed that "he that believeth on me, the works that I do shall he do also" (John 14:12). We know that we are not doing the works that He did; and according to Him our failure is due to a lack of faith. How can one believe when he lives in a constant state of disobedience?

In the first part of this chapter, our disobedience is clearly revealed, and now we see the consequences in our inability to perform His works. How can we perform such works when we have no faith for obedience?

In the light of the facts, it is little wonder that James tells us that "the husbandman waiteth for the precious fruit . . . and hath long patience for it." Such fruit is hard to come by. This must be a source of great anguish to the Master, for it is the dagger of doubt piercing His very heart. It is the setting to our seal that God is not true.

It appears to me that it is high time that I reappraise my love for God that leads to obedience and issues in faith; such faith as He speaks of I do not possess.

Could it be that I do not possess the obedience that makes such faith possible? I would face this issue honestly. There must be an answer, and that answer must lie in truth.

The power of Jesus to convince men lay in the manifestation of His works; His works were more powerful than His words. He said, "Though ye believe not me, believe the works" (John 10:38). And again He said, "If I do not the works of my Father, believe me not" (v. 37). He offered His works as the final proof of His Sonship, and His works convinced many.

The church world is short on the convincing miracle-working power. Faith produces the miraculous, but there can be no such faith without obedience. It might be well to check our obedience to the teachings of the Sermon on the Mount.

Are we like the saints James is telling us of, or are we defending our rights? Are we anxiously facing the future in open disobedience to God's command to "be careful for nothing" (Phil. 4:6)? Do we turn the other cheek? Do we go the second mile? When our goods are taken, do we "ask them not again" (Luke 6:30)? Do we "give to him that asketh" of us?

Can we honestly say that we practice the Sermon on the

Mount? If we cannot say that we do, will we admit that we are building upon the sand, as Jesus said we were?

There is no way that we can practice the teachings of Jesus unless we have faith in Him. Is it the lack of this kind of faith that cuts our effectiveness?

Some of the saints in James's day were practicing the teachings of Jesus, so it must be possible.

Joint-Heirs . . .
if . . . We Suffer

(Rom. 8:17)

One of the most astounding statements in the Word of God is that God's children may become "heirs of God, and joint-heirs with Christ" (Rom. 8:17). Note the "may become." The promise is not a universal one but a conditional one.

Since the possibility is of our being "joint-heirs" with Christ, we should know just what Christ is heir to. The Word does not leave us to guess at this point. The record is clear: "Whom [God] hath appointed heir of all things" (Heb. 1:2). These words are all-inclusive: "all things." No more need be said, but more has been said. This statement is further confirmed by: "Thou hast put all things in subjection under his feet" (2:8). He is "the head of all principality and power" (Col. 2:10). He said, "All things that the Father hath are mine" (John 16:15). More proofs could be added to show that the Father has given all to the Son, but these are sufficient.

His heirship is clear: He has it all, but what does it mean to be a joint-heir? It means to have the same rights as the heir. There is oneness of ownership. Can this be true? It certainly can be. The same God that appointed Christ as "heir of all things" is making possible a joint ownership for others, but this offer is not open to all.

This high honor is open only to those who are "glorified" with Him, and the prerequisite to this glorification is "if so be

58

that we suffer with him" (Rom. 8:17). Jesus won His glory by suffering, suffering that reached to death; and no one else may have such a reward without the same measure of dedication and the same degree of obedience. The acceptance of death for Christ must be real; it may or may not become actual.

Paul must have felt that the "if so be" of the verse might discourage some from pursuing this path of deeper devotion, for he hastens to add, "For I reckon that the sufferings of this present time are not worthy to be compared with the glory which shall be revealed in us" (v. 18).

Paul could speak with some authority of the glory beyond, for he was caught up into the third heaven and saw sights unlawful to be told on earth. In the light of being glorified together with Christ, all earthly suffering paled into insignificance.

There is no virtue in suffering per se. It must have a worthy end, and that end is vividly set forth before us. It is the assurance of the glorious end that lures one on. This was true of Abraham who "looked for a city," of Moses who "endured, as seeing him who is invisible," and of Christ "who for the joy that was set before him endured the cross" (Heb. 11:10, 27; 12:2).

All progress in the Christian life and all rewards in the end are measured by our obedience unto suffering, and obedience unto death must be the accepted lot if one hopes to be a joint heir with Christ. The "if so be" tells us that.

One may well gauge his desire for the high prize of joint heirship by his willingness to suffer. To accept less than the supreme suffering is to close the door to the supreme prize. It is that simple. The appropriate question, therefore, is, "What am I willing to suffer for Christ?"

From the beginning of Christ's ministry until the climax of suffering in the end, there was ever-increasing suffering. Not only did He go this route himself, but He marked the same for us if we would aspire for the grand prize He offers to all.

We only fool ourselves when we say that because times have changed, suffering for Christ has either ceased or lessened. God has not changed, the devil has not changed, sin has not changed; and if the war is over, it is because we have ceased to fight.

Suffering grows out of godlikeness. "Yea, and all that will live godly in Christ Jesus shall suffer persecution" (2 Tim. 3:12). There is no "may," or perhaps; here it is "shall." Our godliness must be measured here as well as in other areas.

Without any reasonable doubt, if Christ could return and repeat His life of dedicated living, He would be despised and rejected by the church world at large. He told us that many would say unto Him in that day, "Lord, Lord," but He would not claim them (Matt. 7:22-23). Do you think they would claim Him if He were here today? I think not. Our lack of suffering is a reflection of our lack of godlikeness. No question here.

When one gets a fuller glimpse of what joint heirship with Christ means and thereby sets his affections on things above, and takes no anxious thought for his life, he, by doing so, lays a foundation for misunderstanding and suffering. To live in another world is to be a stranger here. The natural man does not understand the things of God, and they are foolishness to him. It is reasonable to think that the man who is the embodiment of such "foolishness" would be looked upon as foolish, hence subject to suffering.

To assume, as some have, that since we are living in a different age that the real suffering for Christ is past, is to close the door to all godlikeness that would cause suffering. Thus doing, we cease to "press toward the mark for the prize of the high calling of God in Christ Jesus" (Phil. 3:14); and entering heaven with our bundle of "wood, hay, stubble" (1 Cor. 3:12), we will discover that the "prize of the high calling" has been missed. The joint heirship will be won by those who suffer with Him, for it is written, "If we suffer, we shall also reign with him" (2 Tim. 2:12). The high prize goes to those who "loved not their lives unto the death" (Rev. 12:11). Others, approaching heaven with the ashes of their "wood, hay, stubble," may be saved "yet so as by fire" (1 Cor. 3:15).

This age of ease, affluence, and pleasure is set against all that is being said here, and to rebuke it is to invite suffering. It did so in the lifetime of John the Baptist, Christ, and the apostles, and would do so today.

One should never seek suffering. He should seek godlikeness, and suffering is inevitable when we are godlike. In going this way, one must keep fully in mind that our suffering is not worthy to be compared with the glory that is to follow. To be like Christ and to share His eternal riches eternally is a prize too dear to miss.

It should be remembered that a most dedicated saint "suffered the loss of all things" for Christ and counted those things as dung (Phil. 3:8). He had the proper perspective and made the correct appraisal. No wonder he could say, "None of these things move me" (Acts 20:24). His life was on the altar, His soul in God's hands, His destiny sure, His joint heirship awaiting him.

Hereunto Were Ye Called

(1 Pet. 2:21)

We are called unto holiness; the Word makes that clear. We preach it and sing our much-loved songs concerning it, such as "Called unto Holiness." Such emphasis is good and necessary; but equally necessary is the emphasis upon our call unto suffering.

Peter reminds us that "Christ also suffered for us, leaving us an example, that ye should follow his steps" (1 Pet. 2:21). He also affirms that "hereunto were ye called."

The most certain consequence of Christlikeness is suffering. The word is "Yea, and all that will live godly in Christ Jesus shall suffer persecution" (2 Tim. 3:12). This is a universal statement, and stated differently it reads, "If one suffers no persecution, he is not living godly in Christ Jesus." It is that simple, and here is the divine yardstick by which one's Christlikeness must be measured.

No one who reads the record can deny the fact that Jesus suffered. He suffered at the hands of the Jews, at the hands of His followers, and at the hands of the devil. He was preeminently a sufferer, and Peter said that Christ is an example for us in this area. Our following should be examined.

The Christian's unwillingness to suffer is one of the, if not the most, prolific causes of unchristlikeness, and yet our call to thus suffer is a call from God—a call we cannot reject and be like Christ. But a cursory examination of the reasons for the historical breakdowns in Christianity will reveal the fact that they were caused by man's unwillingness to suffer.

62

John tells us that "among the chief rulers also many believed on him; but because of the Pharisees they did not confess him, lest they should be put out of the synagogue" (John 12:42). The price was too high, the suffering too great.

The parents of the man who was born blind and was healed by Jesus refused to comment on it because "they feared the Jews" (John 9:22). The suffering would be too great.

Paul tells us of false teachers who "constrain you to be circumcised; only lest they should suffer persecution" (Gal. 6:12). Paul also points out that he suffered persecution because he preached that circumcision was not necessary.

Paul joined with Peter in declaring that suffering is a divine call. He wrote the church at Philippi: "Unto you it is given in the behalf of Christ, not only to believe on him, but also to suffer for his sake" (1:29).

Peter reminds us that "forasmuch then as Christ hath suffered for us in the flesh, arm yourselves likewise with the same mind" (1 Pet. 4:1). We are repeatedly reminded that this is a divine call—the Cross stands at the center of the Christian life. The appeal is written in large and living letters. The Hebrews letter tells us, "Jesus . . . suffered without the gate. Let us go forth therefore unto him without the camp, bearing his reproach" (13:12-13).

While many refused to follow Christ because of the suffering, those who do follow Him rejoice in it. When the early disciples were persecuted for Christ's sake, they rejoiced "that they were counted worthy to suffer shame for his name" (Acts 5:41).

Paul affirmed that he "glor[ied] in tribulations." He realized that the suffering and the glory were inseparable: "If . . . we suffer with him, that we may be also glorified together" (Rom. 5:3; 8:17).

Christ taught us, "Blessed are ye, when men shall revile you, and persecute you . . . for my sake" (Matt. 5:11). The dedication of a Christian is revealed when he welcomes suffering, for by suffering for Christ's sake his heavenly reward is thereby increased.

Needless to say that the more closely one walks with Christ, the more keenly will he suffer for Him, for it is this oneness with Him that is the cause of the suffering. Check the life of Jesus, and you will find that the point of His suffering was when He announced His oneness with God. It was the supernatural in His life that antagonized the Jews, and it is the spiritual in the Christian that produces suffering.

This call to suffer, if accepted, may appear in many areas. In the life of Jesus it is seen in connection with His family. His brethren did not "believe in him," and this would be a point of suffering (John 7:5). "His own received him not" (1:11); that would be a point of suffering. His preaching ran counter to that of the scribes and teachers of the law; that, too, would be a point of suffering.

The slowness of His own disciples to comprehend His message would cause suffering, and the lack of faith in Him caused Him grief and pain.

Jesus was very open to remind His would-be followers of the suffering involved. He pictured it in its most realistic terms, reminding them that some of them would be "put to death. And ye shall be hated of all men for my name's sake" (Matt. 10:21-22; Mark 13:12-13; Luke 21:16-17). He added, "A man's foes shall be they of his own household" (Matt. 10:36).

When His disciples asked for position, He asked them if they were able to drink the cup that He must drink, and assured them that the drinking on their part was prerequisite to any seating by Him on His throne.

Jesus never veiled the Cross, covered the bitter cup, or hid the possible worst. He accepted suffering for himself and demanded it for others. He sought the highest rewards for His own, and the path of suffering led always to them.

It was in the suffering, and in it alone, that the glory of God could be best revealed. It has been thus in all ages. Job is an Old Testament illustration. Paul is one from the New. He affirmed, "When I am weak, then am I strong" (2 Cor. 12:10), and through suffering he was able to reveal the grace of God. It has always been thus. The graces of God are seen more clearly in the sufferings of life, and Paul sought the glory of God; hence, he said, "Now also Christ shall be magnified in my body, whether it be by life, or by death" (Phil. 1:20).

God had told him that His strength was made perfect in weakness; therefore Paul gloried in his weakness.

The call is a call to the exaltation of Christ.

The Glory of Weakness

I had just been lamenting my weakness, just a general weakness of spirit, a kind of spiritual weakness that incapacitates one for good Christian service—so I thought. Then suddenly the words came to me, the words of Jesus to Paul, "My strength is made perfect in weakness" (2 Cor. 12:9), and I realized that I was just getting in good shape for the Lord to be made more manifest in me.

Weakness is glorious, for it is, or can be, the forerunner of divine action. It is the recession of the human that the divine may enter. I therefore laud the coming of weakness. I see that Paul did the same; when he saw that the perfection of Christ's strength was rising from the ashes of his own, he exclaimed, "Most gladly therefore will I rather glory in my infirmities, that the power of Christ may rest upon me." The 10th verse delineates his exultation at the thought that such glorious results could come from sources that seemed to be destructive.

He had discovered the secret: "When I am weak, then am I strong"—weak in self, strong in Him. It was then but a short step to his "I can do all things through Christ which strengtheneth me" (Phil. 4:13).

This weakness to strength is the pattern of the Christ-life. He said, "I can of mine own self do nothing" (John 5:30), but He later affirmed, "All power is given unto me in heaven and in earth" (Matt. 28:18). His emptying was complete, His filling was full; in death He lived. This is the pattern for us as it was for Him.

This principle was illustrated in the lives of some Old

Testament saints who "out of weakness were made strong" (Heb. 11:34). Weakness is the condition of strength, and our lack of confessed weakness closes the door to strength. It is our self-sufficiency that closes the door to His efficiency.

If one could only realize that the hour of his weakness was the hour for His exaltation, life would become more radiant and useful.

When Jesus announced, "The hour is come, that the Son of man should be glorified" (John 12:23), He was not thinking of the crown of gold, but the crown of thorns. He was speaking of the corn of wheat that must fall into the ground and die before its fruits could appear, for "he was crucified through weakness, yet he liveth by the power of God" (2 Cor. 13:4). Note the word "liveth." He now lives by the power of Another and not His own. The Father is the Source of all His strength, and His reliance on Him is perfect; hence His perfect power.

The apostle adds the significant statement, "We also are weak in him." Here we come to the crux of the whole matter. Our failure lies in our unwillingness to accept our helplessness, and our strength lies in our weakness. Pride and self-sufficiency block the road to power and usefulness. Self-emptying is the indispensable prerequisite to the divine infilling. It is by the losing of our lives that we save them. It is in dying that we live.

All of these principles we see clearly exemplified in the life of the Master who bids us follow—follow in the full confidence that if we follow Him through the suffering we will share with Him in the glory.

There is nothing impractical about this manner of life. In fact, it is most practical and desirable. Such a person is not envious of another, is not ambitious for position or honor, is not easily hurt at the slights of others. In short, he is easy to live with, for he lives with ease, the ease of One who lives within.

It is needless to say that this pattern of life is foolishness to the man of the world. He is self-assertive, self-seeking, and self-loving. He strains for preeminence and hesitates not to trample his fellowmen beneath his feet in the pursuit of his own aggrandizement. His goal is selfish: He saves himself; others he does not save.

Should this weakness enjoined by God and possessed by Jesus, seem to be beneath the dignity of man, be it remembered that "the weakness of God is stronger than men" (1 Cor. 1:25). When ambitious, boastful, and proud man has reached his most towering pinnacle of success, and like the Babylonian king, boasts, "Is not this great Babylon, that I have built?" (Dan. 4:30), it is then that the Voice from heaven reminds him that his kingdom must fade away.

One of the most prolific causes of human failure is man's unwillingness to admit his helplessness. In the day of tremendous exploitations by man in various realms of nature, and the penetration of the processes of the mind, as well as of nature and the starry heavens, it is quite common to feel no need of God.

As in all other cases, we find the true pattern of life in Him who is Life. He did not shun weakness and explored it even in the hour of His death. He yielded to death that He might destroy him who had the power of death. In the yielding, He conquered; in dying, He lived.

Strange paradoxes these! They would have no meaning but for the fact that God stands ready to make them work. Out of the demise of the human arises the flower of the divine; from the dust of the temporal comes the palace of the eternal. By the alchemy of faith the lost becomes the gained, the surrendered becomes the possessed, and the servant becomes a king.

In the hour of these transmutations, the glory of weakness beams more brightly; the last has become first; the promised has become possessed.

To go the way with the weak is to sit at last with the Victor. The Master has declared it, and time will reveal it.

Godliness and Persecution, the Siamese Twins

Medical skills and techniques have made possible the successful separation of Siamese twins. But there is a set of twins that cannot be separated. God has united them, and what God has united man cannot separate.

Godlikeness and persecution cannot be separated; that is, if God's Word is true, for it reads, "Yea, and all that will live godly in Christ Jesus shall suffer persecution" (2 Tim. 3:12). Note the "all," and that does not mean some. This is an universal statement and applies to every age where men are living godlike lives.

I have had professed Christians tell me that "times have changed" and Christians are not persecuted anymore. My answer is if persecution has ceased, godlikeness has ceased. It may be professed; that does not make it true. Many will say, "Lord, Lord," but will be shut out; so will all those who are hail-fellows with the world.

Christlikeness cannot escape persecution in a sinful world; that is, if Christ told the truth, and He ought to know. Here is what He said: "If the world hate you, ye know that it hated me before it hated you" (John 15:18).

This hatred from the world comes to the saint, not because he is a crackpot or screwball, but because he is like Christ. Christlikeness produces hatred and persecution; it always has and always will. This is true of all who "will live godly in Christ Jesus."

There was a time when Christ's disciples were not hated. Jesus said of them, "The world cannot hate you; but me it hateth, because I testify of it, that the works thereof are evil" (John 7:7).

Why should the world hate them? Take Peter, for example; when the test came, he cursed and swore that he never knew Christ. He catered to the mob and denied his Lord. Why should they persecute him?

Jesus said He was persecuted by the world because He testified against them. He even faced the religious leaders and said, "Woe unto you, . . . hypocrites!" He accused them of being "whited sepulchres, . . . full of dead men's bones" (Matt. 23:13-39); and they sought to kill Him.

After Pentecost, when the Holy Spirit that was *with* them had gotten *in* them, the story was different. Peter boldly accused the Jews of crucifying the Lord of glory, and they eventually killed him. Stephen faced the unbelievers and said, "Ye stiffnecked and uncircumcised in heart and ears, ye do always resist the Holy Ghost" (Acts 7:51); and they stoned him. Typical of Paul's boldness were his words to Elymas, the sorcerer, "O full of all subtilty . . . thou child of the devil . . . enemy of all righteousness" (13:10). He stood against evil, and they beheaded him.

The only way one can escape persecution in this sinful world is to compromise Christlikeness. "In the world ye shall have tribulation" (John 16:33). The Christian does not seek persecution. He seeks to be like Christ, and persecution inevitably follows.

When one compromises Christlikeness to avoid persecution, he also misses the blessedness promised to the persecuted in this life and forfeits his rights to reign with Christ eternally.

The hatred of the holy by the sinful is no new thing, nor

is it a passing sentiment that vanished with Jesus and His disciples. It was the moving passion that caused the first murder. Cain slew his brother, Abel. John asks, "Wherefore slew he him?" What caused this dastardly deed? He answers, "Because his own works were evil, and his brother's righteous" (1 John 3:12).

This deep-seated, universal hatred of the righteous by the wicked was established by God and will last as long as God lasts. In Eden, God said to the serpent, "I will put enmity between thee and the woman, and between thy seed and her seed" (Gen. 3:15). God set the battle lines, and the war will continue to the end, unless we compromise. The compromising professor can escape suffering for Christ, but by so doing he crucifies Christ afresh and puts Him to an open shame.

Should any doubt the continuation of this suffering, let him read the gory pages of the saints' last earthly history and listen to the cry of the martyred saints under the altar. Some are coming up through great tribulation and are making their garments white in the blood of the Lamb.

Someone asks, Then why are we Christians so free from persecution now? The answer has been given to us by God and recorded in Rev. 3:16-17. Never before could it be so truly said of us, Thou art "increased with goods, and have need of nothing; and knowest not that thou art wretched, and miserable, and poor, and blind, and naked."

What is God's proffered solution of the tragic situation? "I counsel thee to buy of me gold tried in the fire" (v. 18), this very fire that we have been dodging because we have been unwilling to be Christlike.

God has always been choosing those who would suffer with Him. When one becomes a prophet of God—not a peddler of the best thinking of men, but speaking "as the oracles of God" (for thus he is commanded)—he may expect suffering. The Bible says, "Which of the prophets have not your fathers persecuted?" (Acts 7:52).

'I have chosen thee in the furnace of affliction" (Isa. 48:10). We will be chosen no other way, for God chooses the Christlike, and He knew the fires of the furnace. We have no promise of reigning with Him unless we suffer with Him.

To these truths I append my testimony and express my deepest desire, expressed earlier by the apostle Paul, "That I may know him . . . and the fellowship of his sufferings" (Phil. 3:10), for "Blessed are ye, when men shall revile you, and persecute you . . . for my sake. Rejoice, and be exceeding glad: for great is your reward in heaven" (Matt. 5:11-12). I seek that blessedness and eternal reward.

What Did My Heart Say?

The question of my title is asked against the background of this statement of the Psalmist: "When thou saidst, Seek ye my face; my heart said unto thee, Thy face, Lord, will I seek" (Ps. 27:8). This is a most important question, for on its answer hangs the divine appraisal of our souls and our true relationship with Him. No other answer is final. The answer of the heart eclipses all others, and by its verdict we rise or fall. I ask myself this question and will face frankly and with perfect honesty the true answer of my heart.

Many answers have been given to the wooing Spirit, answers that come from the lips but do not reveal the true self; hence, they are worthless and self-deceiving. Such answers are those referred to by Jesus when He said of some, "They say, and do not" (Matt. 23:3); or when He said, "This people draweth nigh unto me with their mouth, and honoureth me with their lips; but their heart is far from me" (15:8). Here Jesus is saying that lip honor is meaningless; only the heart response is valid, and the heart was not in this response.

It is interesting to note the reason for this superficial and meaningless response. The next verse reveals the secret: "But in vain they do worship me, teaching for doctrines the commandments of men." Their religion was man-centered and not God-centered. Note, too, that Jesus called them "hypocrites," and hypocrites they were, because their worship was not from the heart. It was but a form of godliness.

It must be noted again and again that insincerity and

73

false profession will populate hell. "And why call ye me, Lord, Lord, and do not the things which I say?" (Luke 6:46). These were stinging but appropriate words from the Master's lips. The words from the heart govern the whole being and reveal the true nature of man, for as a man "thinketh in his heart, so is he" (Prov. 23:7); "Out of [the heart] are the issues of life" (4:23). This matter of the heart response is all-important. Let us again ask the question. "What did my heart say?"

When the gentle, wooing Spirit of God beckoned me to come to be alone with Him, what did I say? From what depth did my answer come? And what was the answer of the heart, although unannounced? So many times I have heard people testify that they had neglected the hour of communion with the Lord, and at other times the complaint was that it was so hard to find time to be with Him. What do such statements add up to? Could it be other than that to be with Him was not the deepest desire of the heart?

If the president of the United States were to give me a personal invitation to spend a half day with him in his Camp David retreat, would I find time to take advantage of the opportunity? Could I make room for time to see a son, returning from a year in the armed forces overseas? Could I find time to visit with my departed mother, should she be raised from the dead and call for me? In short, is there anybody that I would make time to be with?

Who is this Being that is wooing me for fellowship, to whom I so often find little or no time to respond? The Psalmist tells us of Him: "Who is this King of glory? The Lord strong and mighty . . . The Lord of hosts, he is the King of glory" (Ps. 24:8, 10). This is the Personage who woos us, too often in vain, in spite of the fact that the one who seeks His face "shall receive the blessing from the Lord, and righteousness from the God of his salvation" (v. 5). In the light of the majesty of the Being who is wooing us, and the glorious bounties that He has to bestow, how can my neglect be explained?

We must get to the bottom of this matter, lest we be deceived and find ourselves in that vast company who will hear, "I never knew you: depart from me" (Matt. 7:23), at the judgment bar of God. Although it may be painful and self-condemning, I will be as honest as I know how to be in my answer. The Master commanded, "Seek ye first the kingdom of God, and his righteousness; and all these things shall be added unto you" (6:33). This One that has been wooing is the Source and the Giver of righteousness. To those who come to Him, He has promised that they shall "receive . . . blessing . . . and righteousness." If our chief desire and our first seeking is for "his righteousness," why then do we neglect the Source of that which we claim to be our chief desire? If we neglect to be with Him, it is evident that whatever answer we may be giving, and from whatever level of our personality we are speaking, the answer is not coming from our deepest heart when we say that we desire Him above all else.

It is further evident that we do not believe what the Master said when He told us that "all these things shall be added" unto us, if we would seek first His kingdom and righteousness. It is the busy seeking of "these things" that causes us to neglect Him who says that He is the Giver of both righteousness and things. We really are acting on our own judgment and not on His command. This is the central sin of the race: our way as against His.

To add to all the other promises He has given to those who seek His face, He adds this, "The young lions do lack, and suffer hunger: but they that seek the Lord shall not want any good thing" (Ps. 34:10). If this be true, there is indeed a "rest to the people of God" (Heb. 4:9).

Again we are commanded, Cast "all your care upon him; for he careth for you" (1 Pet. 5:7). This sounds so easy. Then why don't we do it? Why all the worry and anxiety? Why do we take (anxious) "thought for the morrow" (Matt. 6:34), when we are commanded not to do so? Why do we not trust Him and be at ease? These are vexing questions, for to answer them honestly is to confess that we do not believe that God is telling the truth. This is the sin of the Israelites that kept them from the Promised Land at Kadesh: "So we see that they could not enter in because of unbelief" (Heb. 3:19).

Let us probe a little deeper. The answer lies beyond. Let us find it, and how may it be found? It can only be found by following the path of truth and honesty. So here we go in the only path that will bring us into more perfect oneness with Him. Do we believe that the Lord was telling us the truth when He said, "He careth for you"? Can we give any credence to His statements in the Sermon on the Mount, such as, "Take no thought, saying, What shall we eat? or, What shall we drink? or, Wherewithal shall we be clothed?" (Matt. 6:31), or "Seek ye first the kingdom of God, and his righteousness; and all these things shall be added unto you" (v. 33)? While speaking on this line, Jesus remarked, "O ye of little faith" (v. 30).

The problem lies in our unbelief, like the unbelief of the Israelites that grieved God; and we are warned to take heed "lest any man fall after the same example of unbelief" (Heb. 4:11). And lest we should overlook a single admonition, the Lord admonishes again, "Take heed, brethren, lest there be in any of you an evil heart of unbelief, in departing from the living God" (3:12). How do we depart from the living God? We are departing when He woos us to seek His face and for reasons that we will mention later, we fail to do so. It is only by closeness with God that we acquire faith to please Him and to believe and obey His commandments.

Going still deeper into the problem, Why do we not draw nigh to Him and become so acquainted with Him that we can find strength to believe and obey? The answer here is the agelong problem of man's unwillingness to submit himself to God's way of life and to meet Him on His terms. It is noteworthy that the key to our failure is found in connection with His command to cast "all your care upon him; for he careth for you," a promise difficult to believe. In the verse immediately preceding this promise (1 Pet. 5:6), we are commanded: "Humble yourselves therefore under the mighty hand of God." This means to accept His will and His pattern for our lives. When we do this, we open the way to remove the perennial excuse for the lack of time to be alone with the Master.

The wonderful promises of His care that we have quoted above, and many others, are based upon our following His pattern of life prescribed for us. The pattern of life that Jesus lived and prescribed for His own is the one that He proposes to underwrite. In a nutshell, God expresses it thus: "Having food and raiment let us be therewith content" (1 Tim. 6:8). God proposes to underwrite our needs but not our wants, the necessities but not the luxuries of life. Our happiness is to emanate from godlikeness and not from the possessions of earth that perish, for "godliness with contentment is great gain" (v. 6).

Jesus warned us of the deceitfulness of riches, and Paul, after telling Timothy, his son in the gospel, about the ones who coveted after money and "erred from the faith, and pierced themselves through with many sorrows," warned him, "But thou, O man of God, flee these things; and follow after righteousness" (1 Tim. 6:10-11).

In the Sermon on the Mount, Jesus referred to "meat" and "raiment" and said, "Your heavenly Father knoweth that ye have need of all these things" (Matt. 6:25, 32). The time that we take working for the things that are not necessary consumes the time that God would like for us to spend with Him. We choose the luxuries of life above the wonders of His fellowship. Things, and not a Person, become our obsession, and the heart of Him who bled for us bleeds on while we frolic and clamor for more of the perishing.

I conclude this chapter as I began it, asking myself the question, "What did my heart say?" when He wooed me to seek His face. The answer that I would make if I were standing in the judgment where all sham and insincerity are melted in the light of the face of Him who is the Truth, would be (and I give it here): Many, many times when You called I was too busy with "Your work" and mine to respond. I cannot change this answer and be honest. I can only "come boldly unto the throne of grace" (Heb. 4:16) and receive pardon! That I do; forgiveness I have.

While I cannot change the answer concerning the past, I can determine the answer of the now; and it is: "Thy face, Lord, will I seek." Amen.

God Planted Both Trees

God planted both trees—the tree of life and the tree of knowledge of good and evil—in the Garden of Eden. I would not have done so; I am quite sure of that. Admitting that He was right when He assured us that His ways are higher than our ways, I know that I would have been wrong in refusing to plant the tree that gave the possibility of evil; but since He did it, I have sought to find the reason for it.

It is evident from the text that the planting of these two trees was purposeful. Earlier in creation, God had "created . . . every plant of the field" and then created man, and then "planted a garden eastward in Eden." There He placed man and caused to grow in the garden "every tree that is pleasant to the sight, and good for food; the tree of life also in the midst of the garden, and the tree of knowledge of good and evil" (Gen. 2:4-9).

The question immediately arises, Why did God plant the tree of knowledge of good and evil in this Edenic garden? It was used as the instrument of man's destruction. Why place it before him? To understand this more fully, one must know something of God's purpose with free moral agency that resulted in the split in heaven.

The unbending law of the universe is the sovereignty of the Father, acknowledged and expressed by full and absolute obedience. The first test known to man, of the free moral agency in the universe, was made in heaven. When that freedom was exercised, Lucifer and many heavenly beings fol-

79

lowing used their freedom for self-exaltation and were cast out.

Testing is a prerequisite to safety and dependability. No car manufacturer would market an untested car. The law will not allow an untested drug to be sold. We depend upon fire to burn, for it has been tested. A sharp knife will cut a finger; my scars prove that. In like manner, the free will of man must be tested. The supreme test is, Will man have his own way, or will he yield himself in full obedience to the will of God?

God made man for eternal fellowship, and man's obedience is an inexorable law of that fellowship. Man must be tested. He must not go untried into the presence of God and his heavenly home; hence, the tree of testing. The basis of the test was the command, "Ye shall not eat of it, neither shall ye touch it, lest ye die" (Gen. 3:3). This was the command of God known to Eve and quoted by her to the devil. She knew both the command and the penalty for its violation. This she admitted before the act of disobedience.

The planting of the tree teaches us many and valuable lessons. It teaches there is no virtue in obedience if disobedience is impossible, and God set before man at the very beginning the means of his own disobedience. To have removed from man the possibility of disobedience would have defeated the very purpose of God. God's desire is for a free obedience; hence the alternative of disobedence must be present. God did make His command clear, and He told man frankly and plainly just what the consequences of disobedience would be.

Another lesson we learn from God's way is that if one obeys, no outside object, circumstance, or tempter can destroy him. The determining factor of the test is within man, and nowhere else. The occasion of sin may be outside, but the cause is invariably on the inside. Because of this, God always deals with the cause and not the occasion. In fact, He is responsible for the occasion. He planted the tree, and He

80

let the devil run loose and tempt man. He could have banished the devil before He made man. He will banish him later, and it is folly to think that He could not have done so earlier.

We may never know God's design in leaving the tempter around until He has closed the human race, but He has. The devil will not be put into his abode—the bottomless pit—until humanity's race has been fully run. It might not be amiss to think on the matter for a moment, using facts that we know to reach a reasonable answer, although Scripture is silent at this point.

We may be sure that disobedience was a possibility in man, even if there had been no outside tempter. Freedom of will implies the possibility of both obedience and disobedience. This is inherent in freedom, and God made angels and man free. He seeks the loving obedience of a freely tested will. It is evident that the test came sooner with the devil's presence and temptation, and perhaps an early testing was more desirable to God than a delayed one. We may well suppose that perfect harmony reigned in heaven for aeons, for aught we know. It is certain that the division was not a created one—the possibility, yes; the fact, no. This grew out of the angels' freedom. The devil's presence would hasten the day of testing and determine the free loyalty of His creatures in the face of possible and suggested disobedience. (*Note:* I am not necessarily committed to the thinking in the preceding paragraph. It is inserted just to stimulate thought on the matter, which to me is not clear.)

The Eden story illustrates the power and the finality of the human will in determining one's own destiny. From the very beginning God was "not willing that any should perish" (2 Pet. 3:9), but the execution of His will was powerless against the execution of man's free will. Paul reminds us "that to whom ye yield yourselves servants to obey, his servants ye are to whom ye obey" (Rom. 6:16). Note, the yielding is the power of the individual. Neither man, the devil, nor another can yield one's will to God or the devil. Upon this fact rests the justice of man's eternal punishment if he yields to sin. Only the one who has the final decision in the matter can justly bear the consequences of the act.

Both trees were planted that man might exercise his God-given power of choice. He exercised it, and that contrary to God's expressed desire. He must bear the full responsibility for his free act. True, he was influenced both by God and the devil. God erected a strong barrier to ruin by explaining the ultimate consequences of self-will against God's command. The devil used the power of persuasive reason, and man followed the reasoning of the devil and disobeyed the command of God.

The Eden story illustrates the power of external forces—God's and the devil's—but neither can draw from man a decision that is not his; and in the final analysis the decision is his, and his alone. The tree of knowledge of good and evil, the deceitfulness of sin, and Satan are ever before us, and so are the commands of God and His warnings of the consequences of disobedience; but neither can elicit a decision from man that is not freely made by him. The tree and the command are necessary; they are ever before us, but we govern the choice that we make between them.